Simply Sourdough

Simply Sourdough

**Baking great whole-grain breads
and more**

Lory Widmer Hess

Simply Sourdough: Baking great whole-grain breads and more
Second edition © 2019 Lory Hess
ISBN 978-1-936849-51-2

The essay "Baking Day" originally appeared in LILIPOH, Fall 2013

Published by the Waldorf Early Childhood Association of North America,
285 Hungry Hollow Rd., Spring Valley, New York 10977, **waldorfearlychildhood.org**.
Visit our online store at **store.waldorfearlychildhood.org**.

This publication was made possible by a grant from the Waldorf Curriculum Fund.

Contents

The What, Why and How of Sourdough

What Is Sourdough?

Sourdough bread is made from dough that has been transformed by the activity of wild yeast. Wild yeast is a single-celled microorganism in the fungus family that goes by the Latin name saccharomyces exiguus, a general term for countless strains that vary from location to location. These strains of yeast exist everywhere in nature, on the surfaces of grains, fruits, and vegetables, and also in the air and on surfaces in your kitchen. A sourdough "starter" is a medium, usually consisting of just flour and water, for capturing and cultivating these wild yeasts into a lively, bubbly mass that will then work on a larger amount of flour, water and other ingredients to leaven bread, or sometimes merely to flavor and condition it.

The "sour" in sourdough comes from lactic acid (also found in lacto-fermented foods such as yogurt and sauerkraut) and acetic acid (as in vinegar). These acids are produced by bacteria that exist symbiotically with the yeast and create the distinctive flavor profile of naturally leavened breads. Such breads need not be particularly sour; the amount and type of acid produced will vary depending on the ingredients used, the strains of yeast and bacteria present, and the length of time the starter, and subsequently the dough, are left to ferment. Enzyme activity and the interaction of bacteria with other by-products of fermentation further affect the flavor of a finished bread.

As a fermented food, like cheese and wine, sourdough bread is transformed by the activity of microorganisms into something quite different from its original components. The yeast consumes the carbohydrates found in flour, producing alcohol and carbon dioxide, which form pockets within the dough and cause it to inflate. When the finished loaf is placed in the oven, the alcohol expands further under heat, and along with a last burst of yeast activity, causes a final rise before it evaporates.

It is interesting to consider that yeast-raised bread is a food that dies and is resurrected twice. The grain is a seed containing potential for growth and reproduction, but it is broken down by being milled into flour. This then becomes the basis for the life of micro-organisms: yeast and bacteria. In the process of baking they are killed in their turn, but their work has made the grain more tasty and easily digestible for us, enabling us to turn it into new energy, new life. This process has sustained humanity since prehistoric times, and until the introduction of commerical yeast about one hundred years ago, it was usually done with sourdough.

Why Sourdough?

The comparatively recent discovery of the existence of microscopic life—which was unknown for most of the history of bread—led to the development of commercial yeast, which in turn changed how bread was made. Unlike the many strains of wild yeast, which can be quite unpredictable and relatively slow in their activity, commercial yeast consists of just one strain, saccharomyces cervisiae, that has been selected and bred to work quickly and consistently. It is cultivated in sterile vats on a solution of diluted molasses, then skimmed off and dried into the convenient, easily stored and measured form most bakers are familiar with.

The creation of commercial yeast went along with the industrialization of baking, which meant mechanizing, streamlining, and speeding up the process to lower costs and maximize profits. Industrialized mills became better at removing the nutritious bran and germ from grain, leaving behind only the starchy endosperm for quick conversion to sugar. These mills were often superheated for higher speed, damaging the starches so that they could not feed the yeast efficiently and needed an aggressive, fast-acting variety. The machines used for mixing and shaping required a certain kind of dough that was easy to extrude, and quick rising to make overall production time shorter, both of which were conducive to the use of commericial yeast.

Thus we have the mass-produced loaves that line supermarket shelves today, a far cry from the true "staff of life" that naturally leavened bread, made with flour that still retained most of its full nutritional value, once represented. It is often filled with additives: vitamins and minerals to replace those lost in milling, preservatives to prevent staling and molding, dough conditioners and flavor enhancers to cover up the tastelessness of starch that has not been transformed by extended fermentation.

Whole-grain sourdough bread, made with a slower, more hands-on process, needs none of these additives. Soaking and long-term fermentation have facilitated enzyme activity, which makes the nutrients naturally available in the unadulterated grain more available to our digestive systems. Lactic-acid bacteria have had time to work, creating flavor and further digestibility. The higher acidity of sourdough also slows staling and helps prevent the growth of mold, making the bread keep longer. And all of this can be achieved with just flour, water, and salt! Commercial yeast is extremely useful and convenient, and can be used to produce very fine baked goods, but if you are interested in a simple, natural, delicious, inexpensive, and wholesome food that has proven its worth over thousands of years, sourdough is for you.

Today, "artisan" bread baking is exploding in popularity, and the delectable results can be sampled even at some supermarkets. Many artisan bakers are enthusiastic and knowledgable proponents of sourdough, as well as of breads made with a yeasted pre-ferment or "sponge," which use a relatively small amount of yeast and are fermented longer at cooler temperatures for sourdough-like qualities.

If you have such a bakery near you, you'll surely want to sample their wares. However, the price tags attached might motivate you to try making your own at home. You may also be curious to experience for yourself the mysteriously simple-yet-complex process of transforming grain into bread, getting your hands into a tradition that goes back to the dawn of civilization. Or you might be inspired by the fact that there is just nothing that tastes better and feels more nourishing than a freshly-baked loaf that has just come out of your own oven. These were my reasons, but I'd say that any reason that gets you to start making bread baking a part of your life is a good one.

How Do I Make Sourdough?

If you're anything like me, you might be intimidated by the whole idea of baking bread, let alone cultivating your own batch of wild yeast. When I was growing up the only bread in our house came in plastic bags with colorful dots on it, and a whole snow-white loaf could be squashed into a ball that fit in the palm of your hand. No one I knew made bread; I'd never seen or felt bread dough. I had a vague yearning to bake my own, but when I looked at recipes, I worried about everything. Wasn't kneading terribly difficult? How would I get the dough unstuck from my countertop? Would I kill the yeast with water that was one degree off from the right temperature? What if I let the dough rise too little or too long? The possibilities for failure confounded me, and I cut my losses by not even trying.

Many years later, when I was pregnant with my son, the urge to try baking bread came on again. A workshop that allowed me to finally get my hands into some actual dough helped, and I think that the experience of having a child did too. Once the entire existence of another human being depends on you, messing around with some flour and water doesn't seem so intimidating any more. After all, the worst that can happen is that you might have to throw out a batch or two. And as I discovered, with baking as with child-raising, learning to improvise is part of the fun.

I started with commercial yeast and a "sponge" method, but sourdough was intriguing to me. I loved the flavor and was interested in the health benefits. As I became more confident in my baking skills, I began to experiment with a rye starter and various recipes. The thing about having a starter is that you have to use it every week—or throw most of it out, but I couldn't bear that idea—so I got a lot of practice. The results weren't always perfect, but they were usually edible. I started to be less dependent on recipes, and more willing to mix methods or try ideas that weren't in any book. I found a way to fit baking into my life, with results that I and my family both enjoyed— and if I can do it, I'm confident that you can too.

The purpose of this book is to describe a step-by-step method for creating a starter that is easy to make and maintain, and using it to bake a whole-grain loaf that rises well and tastes great. This is my "daily bread" that I bake nearly every week, and the heart of this book. The chapter describing it is full of tips, explanations, and other information that I have gathered. It should be read through carefully and then used as a handbook when you are getting started.

This is followed by recipes for several other baked goods—English muffins, 100% sourdough rye bread, pizza dough, pancakes, muffins, and crackers— that can be made with the same starter. There is also an introductory section on ingredients and equipment, and a concluding list of recommended reading and other sources for information and products.

This is not a comprehensive manual of bread baking in general or sourdough in particular. For that purpose, there are many wonderful resources out there, some of which I have listed in the Recommended Reading list.

You will find these extremely interesting and helpful, but I have found that they can also be confusing, contradictory, or overwhelming. In them, I have read that it is tricky to raise bread with only sourdough and not commercial yeast; that whole grain sourdough breads are inevitably dense and heavy; that rye starters produce too much acid to be effective; that whole grain bread must be kneaded for twenty minutes straight to rise well; that many complicated steps and processes are required to make great bread. All of these statements have been refuted by my own experience, which inspired me to share some of what I have learned with other bakers who might not know how easy and satisfying sourdough baking can be.

"Simply sourdough" means that all the recipes in this book are made with sourdough; that each bread is made with sourdough alone, with no added commercial yeast; and that the goal is to demystify the process of making sourdough and help you to feel confident and successful, so that you too can say, "Sourdough is simple!"

Since I first wrote this little book, it's found its way into the world primarily through the support of the Waldorf Early Childhood Association of North America, which endeavors to nourish young children and the adults who care for them in manifold ways. In gratitude for their important work, all proceeds from this new edition will go to benefit WECAN. I've also added an essay I wrote about how baking and mothering intersected for me, which I hope may resonate with your own experiences, as you enter into this life-enhancing adventure.

And now, let's start baking. . .

 When you see this box, you'll find an answer to some of the questions that come up when baking sourdough.

 This box indicates that some sanity-saving tip or important information to remember is being passed along.

Ingredients and Equipment

A Note on Gluten

You may be surprised to learn that the substance we call "gluten" does not actually exist in wheat, or in any other grain. It is formed out of two of the proteins in wheat that bond together when mixed with water to create the long, stretchy gluten strands that give structure to wheat bread. Some of the amino acids in these proteins are problematic for people who have what is commonly called "gluten" intolerance. Similar amino acids are found in rye, barley, and oats, although only wheat has the particular proteins that combine to make gluten.

Making gluten-free breads with grains other than the ones listed above generally involves using a gum (such as xanthan gum) to create the structure that otherwise would be lacking. The recipes in this book do not cover this method, and are not for the gluten-intolerant. However, I have heard several anecdotes from people who may be reacting to other elements in commercial bread other than the gluten. Some can tolerate freshly ground flour, but not the rancid flour often used in commercial whole-grain bread; others can tolerate breads made with sourdough but not commercial yeast. If you have a mild sensitivity or reaction to factory-made yeast bread, you might give freshly made sourdough bread a try. (Serious conditions such as celiac disease are nothing to mess around with.)

Flour

High quality flour is essential; since these breads are not enriched with sugar or dairy products, the flour is the main element of both flavor and structure.

Whole grain flour begins to go rancid as soon as the fat-containing germ and outer layer of bran are crushed, so if you plan to do a lot of baking, you might want to grind your own for true freshness. A good quality electric mill can be had for around $300 and will pay for itself in time, as you can buy grains in bulk at a discount. If stored properly, unmilled grain will keep for at least several months.

If you prefer or need to use pre-milled flour, there are good options available. Try your local natural foods co-op, if you are lucky enough to have one, and see if they have locally grown or milled flour; failing that, there are some decent commercial brands, and mail order is always an option. Whole-grain flour should be stored in the freezer to preserve freshness and used as soon as possible. Organically grown grains are best for sourdough, as the chemicals used in conventional agriculture discourage the wild yeast you are seeking to cultivate.

Wheat

As described above, gluten is formed from two proteins in wheat flour; when mixed with water these weak proteins bond together to create strong, stretchy strands. Through kneading, the strands are organized into sheets that trap gases formed by fermentation (activity of yeast and bacteria). This is what makes it possible for breads to be light and airy.

No other grain has as much gluten-forming potential as wheat. It is the easiest flour to use for light, high-rising breads. Hard wheat berries have the most protein and are ground into "bread flour," which is generally the most suitable for bread baking, as opposed to the low-protein pastry flour ground from soft wheat berries, and middle-of-the-road all-purpose flour, which is a blend of both. It can be also be mixed with other flours, which lend other qualities. Two of these are described below.

Rye

Rye has one of the gluten-forming proteins, but without the other it cannot achieve the strength of wheat when hydrated, remaining weak and formless. It also contains starches that tend to grab the water and make sticky, wet dough. Rye is easier to work with when mixed with wheat flour, which mitigates these qualities while benefiting from rye's moisture-trapping ability to make moist, flavorful breads. If the ratio of rye to wheat is less than 1:6, the dough should not be overly sticky. More than this and you will need significantly different expectations and techniques than with wheat dough.

In breads made with a large amount of rye, a sourdough or other acid ingredient is needed to help retard enzymes that would break down the fragile, low-gluten structure of the bread. The more acidic the starter, the less leavening power it has, so many bakers add commercial yeast to rye bread to compensate for this. However, it is entirely possible to make a delicious rye loaf without it, as long as you don't expect it to act like wheat bread.

Fortuitously, rye is very easy to use for a sourdough starter; it ferments more quickly than wheat, due to its high starch level. In this book, a 100% rye starter is used. It is also possible to get a starter going using rye, and then switch over to wheat to complete and maintain it.

If you are not grinding your own flour from whole rye berries (which I do and recommend), it can be difficult to tell what you are getting with commerically ground rye flour. "Medium rye flour," which is commonly available, has probably had some of the germ and bran removed. "Dark rye flour" may be whole ground rye, or it may be missing some of the endosperm and germ. "Pumpernickel flour" may be a very coarse whole grain flour, or it may be more finely ground. King Arthur Flour sells an organic pumpernickel flour that is similar to the home-ground flour I prefer.

Spelt

Spelt is an older variety of grain that is closely related to wheat. The proteins it contains act in a way similar to those in wheat, forming a type of gluten that makes a well-structured bread. However, this gluten is more soluble and its structure is more fragile, so it requires careful handling. This type of gluten may be tolerated better by some people who have difficulty with wheat gluten, but it can still be problematic.

Water

Other than flour, water is the main ingredient in your bread, and you may notice different results depending on the water you use.

Use non-chlorinated water when cultivating a starter; chlorine will interfere with the wild yeast you are trying to cultivate. If the only water you have is chlorinated tap water, let it sit in an open pitcher on the counter over-night to evaporate the chlorine. (Increasingly, tap water is being treated with chloramine, a chemical compound of chlorine and ammonia, which does not dissipate readily; check with your town to see if this is the case with your water.) You can also use bottled spring water. Water that has had its minerals removed by a filter will not work as well; a certain level of mineral content helps nourish the yeast.

Once you have a healthy starter going, you may be able to use your tap water, but if your starter acts sluggish, try eliminating the chlorine again.

Whole grain flours absorb much more water than white flour, which requires some getting used to if you are accustomed to baking white breads. Whole grain flour is also affected by the humidity in the air, so your bread may need much less water added to it in a humid climate. The water is easier to adjust if the flour is measured first and water is added to it gradually, rather than the other way around.

The water you add to your starter or dough should be about room temperature, not warm as in yeast recipes, and not icy cold.

Salt

Salt plays an amazing number of roles in bread. It chemically strengthens the gluten structure so that the dough becomes bouncy and resilient, rather than remaining slack and formless. It holds back yeast activity so that the dough does not get too acidic before it has risen well. It gives starches a chance to break down into sugars that form the characteristic caramelized brown crust. It holds onto moisture, slowing staling. And of course, it enhances flavor. If you forget to add salt to your dough you will end up with sticky, flabby dough and bland, pale bread.

Salt used in bread should be high quality, with no iodine or other additives. Sea salt, kosher salt, and non-iodized table salt will all work. (Do not use coarse salt, as it will not dissolve quickly enough.) Finely ground sea salt was used in developing these recipes.

Time (and Temperature)

It may seem odd to think of time as an ingredient, but it is the only other element you need—aside from flour, salt, and water—to make great bread, and it is equally important. The time spent in making bread is more about letting things happen and watching for the right moment to move to the next step, than lots and lots of hands-on activity. It is also quite flexible, depending on the temperature, with which it is in a direct relationship. For either the rising or proofing stages, you can cool down your dough (in the refrigerator, for example), to slow its activity and make it fit better into your schedule.

Now, I usually set up my starter in the evening and finish the bread over the course of the next day, but when I had a young toddler running around, I used to make my starter in the morning, mix and knead my dough in the evening (so I could get my hands sticky without worrying about what he was up to), let it rise overnight in the fridge, and do the final steps the following afternoon around naptime. Several suggested time-lines are given in "Timing Your Baking."

In general, longer fermentation at relatively low temperatures gives better tasting and better keeping breads. Medium room temperature (70-74°F) works well in most cases and was used to calculate the times in these recipes. If the temperature goes below or above this range, the times will need to be adjusted (longer or shorter, respectively).

Other factors such as the liveliness of your starter and the amount of moisture in the dough can also affect your bread's behavior. Keep in mind that the times given in this book are just a starting point for your own observation. As you become more experienced with baking, you will learn to recognize the signs that your dough is ready to move on to the next stage, and become less dependent on the clock.

Packaged and Passed-Down Starters

You can use a packaged starter if you wish, but it's fun and fascinating (like a fourth-grade science project) to make your own from scratch.

Some starters have gathered an incredible mystique about them, giving the impression that they have uniquely effective culturing organisms that have been handed down from the depths of antiquity, but be aware that once you have used and refreshed them several times most of the wild yeast will be coming from the fresh flour you add and the air in your kitchen.

The same goes for the starter that you get from a friend or neighbor that was started by her great-grandmother. Some people are so intimidated by the need to keep an heirloom starter persisting for all eternity that it puts them off sourdough baking altogether. If you're lucky enough to receive such a gift you can definitely use it, but don't worry if it doesn't survive and you have to start a new one. (You can always hand that one down to your great-grandchildren.)

Some bakers even say that "old" starters are not necessarily ideal, routinely throwing theirs out and starting with a fresh one periodically, as acids and unhelpful organisms can build up over time. This is another realm for you to experiment in and find what works for you.

Recommended Equipment

To bake sourdough bread you really need only basic kitchen equipment: a container with a lid for the starter, a couple of large bowls (ceramic or glass, ideally), tea towels or plastic wrap, measuring cups and spoons, spatulas and wooden spoons, and so on. Some often-recommended additional items that you might not already own are listed below.

An oven thermometer is inexpensive, and will give you a better idea of the actual temperature of your oven than the dial.

A good digital scale is nearly essential. Weighing is much more accurate than measuring by volume, for both dry and liquid ingredients. A scale that reads in both ounces and grams is the most versatile. It should have a tare feature and measure in increments of at least $1/8$ to $1/10$ of an ounce. I also use mine to help interpret European recipes, as a postage scale, for weighing fruit for jam making, and more, so it was definitely worth the cost (expect to spend $25 to $50).

Unless you have access to a local mill, a grain grinder is essential if you want truly fresh flour. If you don't have the will- and muscle-power to grind by hand, an electric mill is what you want for the quantities needed for bread. It's important that your mill not over-heat the flour, which will compromise its quality.

A cast iron pan can be heated in the oven with water to produce steam, which helps keep the crust of the loaf soft until it has reached its maximum expansion. The treatment will ruin the pan for other purposes, so reserve one for this use.

A baking stone is not required for the recipes in this book, but you will find it discussed in many of the "recommended reading" books, and you may wish to try one. It gives strong, even heat that helps breads to rise well, but requires extra heating time. The cast iron pan I suggest putting in the oven partially fills this function, but the baking stone gives heat directly to the bottom of the bread, especially important when making pizza or hearth loaves without a pan.

Creating the Rye Mother Starter

A sourdough starter cultivates the yeast that is found naturally on the surface of whole grains and in the air. Organic grains and non-chlorinated water are best for this, to help keep chemicals away from the yeast until it is well established.

Once you have a "mother starter" going, you can keep it indefinitely in your fridge, using part of it to make the starter for bread and adding more flour and water to refresh the small amount that is left.

You will often hear this refreshing called "feeding," but this is not a completely accurate description of what is happening. You are enlivening the starter as much by adding fresh and hungry yeast, as by giving it something to eat. However, it's hard to avoid the impression that in tending a starter one is caring for a small pet (fortunately a not terribly demanding one).

Using a clear, straight-sided plastic or glass container with a lid makes it easiest to see and measure the activity of the starter. Surfaces (bowls, containers, utensils, etc.) should be clean but free of soap residue to avoid damaging the yeast. A one-to-two-quart container gives plenty of space for the starter to expand.

With quick-fermenting rye flour, it can take only a few days to make an active starter. If it takes longer, though, don't give up. Many factors can affect the activity of your starter, and there's nothing wrong with taking more time if you need it.

Day 1

Stir together 4 fluid oz. (½ cup) water and 3 oz. (⅔ cup) rye flour in your container. Cover and keep at warm room temperature (ideally 74–80 degrees) for 24 hours, stirring once with a wet spatula during that time if possible.

 Sometimes a certain type of bacterial activity can interfere with yeast development. Stirring the starter once a day helps the yeast to grow faster and overcome the bacteria.

Day 2

Add 4 fluid oz. (½ cup) water and 3 oz. (⅔ cup) rye flour to your container and stir the mixture. Cover and keep at warm room temperature again for 24 hours (stirring once if possible).

Day 3

The mixture should be bubbly and have expanded, with a sour taste and smell. Add 4 fluid oz. (½ cup) water and 3 oz. (⅔ cup) rye flour and stir. Cover and keep at warm room temperature again for 24 hours (stirring once if possible).

 More time may be needed to give the yeast a chance. If activity seems to come to a halt after the third day, keep adding flour and water for a few more days. If the volume gets too large for your container, discard some and keep going.

Day 4 and beyond

The mixture should be very bubbly and have expanded a great deal, perhaps doubled. Add 4 fluid oz. (½ cup) water and 3 oz. (⅔ cup) rye flour and stir to break up the air bubbles. Scrape down the sides and mark the level of the mixture on the container with a marker or a strip of tape. Cover and keep at warm room temperature again for only 8 hours.

If the mixture doubles in volume in 8 hours, it is ready to be used. If not, keep going with adding flour and water for a few more days. If the volume gets too large for your container (it should never take up more than half the container after being stirred down and before expansion), discard about half the mixture and just keep going.

Use immediately to make starter for bread according to the instructions in the chapter on "Making the Active Bread Starter." Or, refrigerate it for up to three days. If you haven't used the newly made mother starter within three days, refresh it (see "Refreshing the Mother Starter") and return it to the fridge.

 Your newly made mother starter is still young and will continue to change and develop. Bake with it for a few batches and it should become more strong and active.

Making the Active Bread Starter

Once you have a mother starter, you will remove most of it from its storage container and double its volume with flour and water to make the starter that will raise your bread. This recipe yields 18 oz. / 2 cups of active starter.

8–24 hours (depending on the recipe) before mixing your bread dough, take the rye mother starter out of the fridge. Let it warm and bubble up for an hour or two if possible. Stir it down with a wet spatula. Weigh or measure out 9 oz. / 1 cup of mother starter into a bowl.

 To measure by volume, stir down the starter well with a wet spatula, then measure into a cup that has been rinsed with water to help prevent sticking.

To this bowl, add:

    4 oz. / ½ cup spring water
    5 oz. / 1 cup rye flour

Cover with plastic wrap or a damp towel and allow to ferment at room temperature for the amount of time specified in the recipe.

Refreshing the Mother Starter

After you make the bread starter, there should be a small amount of mother starter remaining in the storage container.

To this, add:

      5 oz. / ½ cup + 2 Tablespoons spring water

      4 oz. / ¾ cup rye flour

Stir well, let stand 1 hour at room temperature if possible, then refrigerate.

Use again or refresh within one week.

Refreshing the mother starter if not baking with it within one week
Once it is established, you should ideally use or refresh the mother starter at least once a week. Using it more often is also fine.

To refresh the mother starter without using it, remove 9 oz. / 1 cup of the mother starter, then add 5 oz. water and 4 oz. flour as above.

 If you don't remove enough of the "old" starter, un-helpful organisms and processes may start to take over. Only a small amount (1 or 2 tablespoons) should ever be kept to mix with the fresh flour and water.

Timing Your Baking

As mentioned in the chapter on "Ingredients and Equipment," you can use time and temperature to adjust bread recipes to suit your own schedule. In general, if you lower the temperature, the bread will take longer to ferment, and you can use this principle to fit the hands-on tasks of baking into your day.

Many different scenarios are possible. Some examples for the Wheat/Rye Sourdough Bread:

> DAY ONE: Make starter and soaker at 9 pm—DAY TWO: Mix at 7 am—Knead with rest periods from 7:20 am to 8 am—Shape at 2 pm—Bake in a cold oven at 3:30 pm—Done at 4:45 pm

> DAY ONE: Make starter and soaker at 9 am—Mix at 9 pm—Knead continuously from 9:10 to 9:30 pm—Put in fridge to rise—DAY TWO: Remove from fridge to warm up at 5 pm—Shape at 7 pm—Bake in a hot oven at 8 pm—Done at 9 pm

> DAY ONE: Make starter and soaker at 6 am—Mix at 4 pm—Knead with rest periods from 4:20 pm to 5 pm—Shape at 11 pm—Put in the fridge to proof—DAY TWO: Remove from fridge to warm up at 6 am—Bake in a cold oven at 7 am—Done at 8:15 am

Don't use the refrigerator for more than one stage, and always wrap the bread very well when refrigerating to keep it from drying out.

Because the whole baking process can take 24 hours or more, it does require some forethought; this is not a last-minute activity. However, once you find a schedule that works for you and fit it into your daily and weekly rhythm, it really is quite possible to have your own homemade bread with less effort than running to the store.

Wheat/Rye Sourdough Bread

Make starter and soaker

8 to 12 hours before you want to start mixing your dough, make 18 oz. of starter according to the instructions for "Making the bread starter."

In a separate bowl, make a "soaker" by mixing:

> 4 oz. / ¾ c. rye flour
>
> 24 oz. / 6 cups whole wheat bread flour
>
> 1 Tablespoon salt

Gradually stir in approximately 500 ml. / 2¼ cups room temperature water. The flour needs to be moist throughout, but not wet; be patient and keep mixing before adding more water. Make sure there are no dry, tough patches.

 Soaking the whole grain flour helps to soften the pieces of bran (which have sharp edges that will cut the gluten strands you are trying to develop), and also to start enzyme activity that will help to release nutrients and more complex flavors. Salt helps to prevent fermentation from starting too soon and interfering with this.

Cover both starter and soaker with plastic wrap or a damp towel and leave at room temperature for 8 to 10 hours or overnight (up to 12 hours if the temperature in the room goes down to 60°F or less).

Mix dough

Measure out about a cup of room temperature water and set aside.

Divide the soaker into small handfuls. Mix into the starter bowl until thoroughly combined (easiest to do by squashing with your fingers), adding about 1 cup white bread flour.

 A small amount of white bread flour, with its strong gluten and high starch content, helps give a better rise. It does not need to be soaked because it doesn't have any bran. You can omit it or add more whole-wheat or rye flour to the soaker if you do not want to use any white flour; adjust the water as necessary.

The dough will be fairly stiff, but well moistened, with no hard clumps. Some loose white flour is fine. If a little more water seems to be needed, sprinkle some in a tablespoon or two at a time, and mix well.

After mixing, it's ideal to allow the dough to rest for 5 to 20 minutes in order to absorb and redistribute the water. After resting, it will be more cohesive and less sticky than if you started to knead right away.

Knead dough

Turn dough out onto counter. Use a little water to keep the dough from sticking by lightly wetting your hands and counter as you knead (which means thoroughly working the dough through by pressing, folding, and turning it). The dough should be very moist but still hold together.

Using water rather than flour to keep the dough from sticking helps keep you from adding too much flour, which makes a dry loaf. Whole-grain flour absorbs more water than white flour and will also react strongly to the level of humidity in the air. Adjust the water used so you end up with a moist but not wet dough.

The usual next step is to knead vigorously for 15 to 18 minutes, observing how the dough changes in texture. It will be sticky and slack at first, but be persistent and it will become more and more smooth and resilient.

While it is very interesting to observe this transformation, for regular baking I recommend a less strenuous method: knead for 5 minutes or so, then cover the dough and let it rest while you do something else for 10 to 20 minutes (cook breakfast, take a shower). Repeat a couple of times and notice how the dough changes while you are not paying attention to it. Magic!

Kneading develops gluten structure, organizing it into sheets that will trap gases like a balloon. However, gluten will develop on its own just through flour sitting in contact with water, or "resting"—though much more slowly.

When the dough is losing its stickiness and becoming smooth and resilient, shape it into a ball. This can be done by gently flattening it, then folding the edges to the inside, forming a smooth surface on the bottom. Pick up the ball, turn it over and pull the edges around to the bottom, further tightening this surface. Let the dough rest covered with a damp cloth while you wash and oil or butter the bowl.

 Soak the bowl first in cold water, not hot, and scrub your hands with cold water and a washcloth before applying soap and warm water. Hot water "bakes" the dough onto surfaces and makes them harder to clean.

Knead a few minutes more, until the dough can be formed into a smooth ball that bounces back quickly when pressed with a wet finger, like a well-inflated balloon.

Ferment the dough

Return dough to the clean, buttered bowl, turn to coat with butter and cover loosely with a damp cloth or plastic wrap. Let rise at room temperature for 5–6 hours. It should have approximately doubled in volume and should now keep an imprint that fills in slowly when pressed with a wet finger. If not, let it rise longer.

If the dough deflates and "sighs" when pressed, it has risen too long. Gently remove it from the bowl, knead briefly and shape into a taut ball again, and let it rise for an hour or so before shaping.

You can use your favorite non-dairy grease for the bowl and pans if you wish. You can also prevent sticking in the bowl with a small amount of water, though this will not work for the pans.

Shape loaves

Gently press the center of the dough with a dampened hand, and pull up the sides to turn out of the bowl. Divide into two equal pieces. Shape these into tight balls and let rest 15 minutes.

 Here, resting allows the gluten (which has been stretched by shaping the dough into balls) to relax before the final shaping into loaves. This helps to give a better rise. You may skip this step if you are short on time.

Gently flatten the balls, using a small amount of water on your hands and surfaces to prevent sticking. Turn over, and shape them into ovals by stretching the top surface around on both sides, somewhat like folding a burrito, and tucking the other two ends to fit. Put into greased loaf pans.

Proof loaves

The final rise is called the "proof" and is always shorter than the other stages. I usually proof for a very short time and put the loaves into a cold oven. This is something that I have never seen recommended by anyone, but my husband suggested it and it actually produced a great rise and a nicely browned crust (besides simplifying things for people like me who tend to forget to preheat the oven at the right time).

 I don't have an authoritative answer, but my theory is that the gradually rising temperature helps to give the yeast a boost before it is killed by the high temperature of baking.

The same result may be achieved by proofing the bread to exactly the right state, and putting it into a very hot oven, causing the celebrated "oven spring"—but you might find that the cold-oven method is simpler and more flexible.

Let your loaves rise in the pans, covered with a damp cloth, in a warm place for 15 to 30 minutes. They will rise slightly but still be quite springy.

Bake loaves (Cold-oven method)

Place a cast iron skillet filled with water on the floor of your oven (if possible) or on the bottom rack. Slash the tops of the two loaves with a serrated knife or sharp razor—one vertical slash or a few diagonal ones, or a cross. Put the loaves on a rack in the center of the oven and turn it to 375°F. Bake for 70 minutes.

 The cast iron skillet adds "heat mass" that helps to keep the heat in your oven consistent. The water creates steam that keeps the crust of the loaf soft in the first part of the baking time, allowing it to rise higher.

When done, the loaves will be browned, release easily from the pans, and sound hollow when tapped on the bottom. If the sound is muffled, bake for 10 minutes more and check again.

Bake loaves (Hot-oven method)

If you want or need to bake in a hot oven (e.g. because it's already hot from some other cooking task), proof the loaves for 45 to 60 minutes, until they have risen to a good dome and the imprint of a wet finger fills in slowly. Put loaves in a 375°F oven and bake for 1 hour.

 You can heat the cast iron pan in the oven, and then carefully add water to it when putting in the loaves. Watch out for the steam! A safer method is to spray water into the oven on first putting the loaves in (avoiding the oven light if you have one, so it doesn't burst), and again after 10 minutes of baking.

Cool loaves

Let cool completely before slicing, at least 2 hours.

 Cutting warm bread releases moisture, which should rather be allowed to settle and redistribute through the loaf as it cools for the most flavorful, best-keeping bread. So resist early slicing if you can!

Storage

Store any bread that you don't eat right away in a paper bag at room temperature. The crust will dry out, but the inside will stay moist for several days and also can be refreshed by toasting. Storage in plastic bags will keep the crust soft but encourages molding, as moisture tends to collect on the inside of the bag. Storage in the fridge tends to dry out the bread. Loaves can also be well wrapped and frozen.

Variations: Adding seeds and spices

Traditional bread spices such as ground coriander, ground or crushed fennel, anise, and caraway seeds, and ground cumin can be added for delicious results. Add a teaspoon or more of each spice to your soaker along with the salt. Adjust quantities to taste.

Seeds—such as sunflower seeds, sesame seeds, and flax seeds—can also be added for extra flavor and nutrition. Seeds must always be soaked separately before adding because otherwise they will draw moisture out of the dough as it bakes.

When you make the soaker, in a separate bowl soak ½ cup of sunflower seeds, sesame seeds, and/or flax seeds in ½ cup water. Drain any unabsorbed water before adding to the dough.

Be sparing when you add water to the dough during the kneading stage, and then work the wet seeds in towards the end. Flax seeds especially will become very slimy and mucilaginous. Add more water at the end if the dough is still stiff.

English Muffins

The dough for Wheat/Rye Sourdough Bread can also be used to make English muffins. One loaf's worth of dough will make 8 to 12 muffins, but you can use a smaller or larger amount.

At the kneading stage, knead in more water than usual until the dough is very wet (but not quite falling apart). The dough will rise faster than usual because it is so wet; let it rise around 4 hours until it retains the imprint of a wet fingertip.

Shape the risen dough into balls (one loaf's worth will make 8 large or 10–12 smaller muffins), then flatten into rounds. Let them rise on a floured board or cookie sheet until they are very well risen and starting to flatten out. This may take 1 hour or more.

Bake on a hot, ungreased griddle for about five minutes, then turn. Keep flipping back and until brown on both sides (but not burnt) and dry on the edges.

Split one with a fork to test doneness.

100% Sourdough Rye

Make starter

12 to 24 hours before you want to mix your bread, make the active starter according to the instructions on page 27. Let sit, covered with plastic wrap or a damp towel (be sure it does not dry out), at room temperature; it should become spongy and quite sour.

WHY? *Rye flour does not contain the same kind of gluten-forming proteins as wheat, and so lacks the structure that gluten gives to wheat bread. In 100% rye bread, an acid ingredient is needed to retard enzymes that would otherwise break down the dough completely into a gooey mess. A sourdough starter that has been fermented for an extra-long time develops acids that help it to play this role. In the process it loses some of its leavening capacity, though, so many bakers add some commercial yeast to compensate. However, this bread can be made successfully without it.*

Mix dough

Measure out about 13 oz. / 1½ cup of starter. Use, give away, or discard remaining starter.

You can use the remaining 5 oz. / ½ cup of starter to make Pumpkin-Nut Sourdough Muffins, or Spelt/Wheat Pizza Dough. Remove and use it after the first 8–12 hours of fermentation.

Stir in: 8 oz. / 1 cup spring water.

Add: 11 oz. / 2¼ cups rye flour

        1½ teaspoons salt

 This rye-only dough does not require kneading to develop the gluten as with wheat breads, and would be unbearably sticky if one tried. A good stirring is all that is required for the batter-like dough.

Rising

Cover with plastic wrap or a damp cloth and let stand till risen by about one third; this may take 1½ to 2 hours or more.

Proof loaf

Put dough in 8 x 4-inch greased pan that has been dusted with rye flour. Let rise until slightly domed, 1 hour or more.

Baking

Heat oven to 325°F (with cast iron skillet on bottom if you wish). Put in bread, carefully add water to cast iron pan (optional), or spray oven with water (avoiding oven light) and bake 2 hours or longer.

Rye flour contains abundant pentosans, starchy substances that trap water like sponges. Because of this, rye dough absorbs more water than wheat dough, and requires a long baking time to ensure it is cooked through.

Cooling

Cool 10 minutes in pan, remove, and cool on rack. It's best to wait 24 hours or more before slicing and eating this dense, moist bread.

Spelt/Wheat Pizza Dough

Make starter

8–10 hours before you want to mix your dough, make the active sourdough starter according to the instructions on page 27 (or use starter from another recipe).

Mix dough

Measure out 5 oz. / heaping ½ cup of active sourdough starter. Use, give away, or discard remaining starter.

You can use the remaining 13 oz. of starter in some of the other recipes in this book, adjusting the proportions, if necessary.

Mix starter with (in this order):

14 oz. / 1¾ cup spring water

13 oz. / 2½ cup white bread flour

13 oz. / 2½ cup whole spelt flour

2 teaspoons salt

Never add salt directly to your starter, because it will interfere with the activity of your yeast. Always buffer it with flour first.

Resting/kneading

Let rest in bowl 15 to 20 minutes to absorb water. Lift the dough and slap it down hard onto the counter for about 5 minutes. Use olive oil on your hands and counter if dough is sticky.

 Slapping the dough on the counter is another way to quickly develop and align the gluten strands. It's especially suited to this soft and rather sticky dough.

 Oil your hands and the counter generously and be patient; stop kneading if the stickiness gets too much. The resting periods will work wonders on the dough.

Rest dough in bowl (clean and oil it first), covered with a damp cloth, for about 20 minutes.

Slap the dough again for 3 to 5 minutes. The dough should become smooth, soft, and elastic.

Rising

Let rise in bowl at room temperature for about 45 minutes, covered with plastic wrap or a damp cloth. Then let it rise in the refrigerator overnight or up to 24 hours (plastic wrap is best for this to avoid drying out the dough).

Adding a stage of long, slow rising in the refrigerator—or "retarding" the dough—helps to develop flavor. Some recommend this particularly for spelt dough, but you can experiment with it for any bread (see "Timing Your Baking")

Shaping, topping and baking

30 minutes to 2 hours before you want to make the pizza, take out the dough to let it warm up. This will take less time if you remove it from the cold bowl and divide it into two pieces which you shape very gently into flat rounds. Keep them covered with plastic wrap or a damp towel.

Heat oven to 450°F. Oil two half-sheet pans. Gently stretch one of the rounds of dough, taking several breaks to let the gluten relax, till it covers the pan.

 When gluten is tensed, it snaps back like a rubber band. This makes it very frustrating to try to stretch the dough continuously, as it will resist you and tear. However, a brief rest lets the gluten relax again and be stretched further.

Lightly spread the pizza with sauce, cheese, vegetables, or other toppings; don't overload it. Bake 15 to 20 minutes, or until crust is done and toppings hot. While one pizza is baking you can prepare the other. The unbaked dough can also be frozen, well wrapped, for later use.

Whole-grain Sourdough Pancakes

Mix starter, flour and liquids

8–10 hours before you want to make pancakes, mix in a bowl:

> 1–4 Tablespoons mother starter or active sourdough starter
>
> 1½ cups flour (any combination of whole grain flours; I like a mix of whole-wheat pastry flour, spelt, and buckwheat. You can mix in some all-purpose flour if you wish.)
>
> 1¼ to 1½ cups buttermilk, or yogurt thinned with milk

Mix and cook final batter

Add to dry ingredients:

> 1 egg
>
> 1 Tablespoon oil
>
> ½ teaspoon salt
>
> ½ teaspoon baking soda
>
> 1 Tablespoon sugar

Stir till combined, then drop onto a hot, greased griddle and cook on both sides till lightly browned.

Makes about 10 medium-sized pancakes. Recipe can easily be doubled to make more.

 You can either steal a bit of mother starter directly from your storage container, adding a little extra flour and water next time you refresh it to compensate, or use some leftover starter from another recipe.

Pumpkin-Nut Sourdough Muffins

Make starter

8-10 hours before mixing the muffins, make the active sourdough starter according to the instructions on page 27 (or use starter from another recipe).

 This recipe uses ½ cup of the active starter; it can easily be doubled to use up more, or the remaining starter can be used in other recipes from this book.

Mix ingredients

In one bowl, thoroughly combine:

> ½ cup (about 4–5 oz) active sourdough starter
>
> 1 cup pumpkin puree (about half of a 15 oz. can)
>
> 2 Tablespoons buttermilk or yogurt
>
> 2 Tablespoons olive oil
>
> 2 eggs
>
> ¼ cup honey
>
> ¼ cup brown sugar or sucanat

In another bowl, whisk together:

> ¾ cup all-purpose flour
>
> ¾ cup whole wheat flour
>
> ¼ teaspoon salt
>
> 1½ teaspoons baking soda
>
> 1 Tablespoon cinnamon

Add the dry ingredients to the moist ones and mix together until just combined.

Stir in 1½ cup chopped walnuts.

Fill muffin tins and bake

Spoon into greased muffin tins, filling about three-quarters full and allow to sit at room temperature for about 30 minutes.

Preheat the oven to 350°F.

Bake for 20 to 25 minutes until done in the center. Cool for 5 minutes in pan, then cool completely on a rack.

Makes one dozen muffins.

Sourdough Crackers

Make starter

8–10 hours before you want to mix the crackers, make the active sourdough starter according to the instructions on page 27 (or use starter from another recipe).

Mix dough

Combine in bowl:

> 9 oz. / 1 cup active sourdough starter
> ⅓ cup melted butter or olive oil

Add 1 cup flour; you may use unbleached white flour, whole grain flour, or a combination. Stir well and add additional flour, if necessary, until you have a stiff dough. Knead the dough in the bowl when it becomes too stiff to stir.

Cover with a damp cloth and set aside at room temperature for at least 8 and up to 24 hours.

Add seasonings

Preheat oven to 350°F.

Remove your dough ball from the bowl and break it up with your fingers. Add ¼ teaspoon salt, ¼ teaspoon baking soda, and your seasoning of choice. This can include dried herbs, garlic, onion or mustard powder, grated cheese, etc. Start with a tablespoon or two or herbs and spices and/or a handful of cheese, and adjust quantities according to taste.

Roll out and bake

Divide the dough in half. Take one half and roll it out onto a lightly greased cookie sheet, or onto a piece of parchment paper that you can then slide onto a cookie sheet. Roll as thinly as you can for crispy crackers. If your dough is very sticky, you can lay a piece of plastic wrap on top.

After the dough is rolled as thin as possible, sprinkle with coarse salt and press in lightly. Cut into small pieces with a sharp knife or pizza cutter. Bake for 15 minutes or until browned and crispy (start checking after 10 minutes).

Cool on rack before storing in a sealed container.

For more crackers, double or triple the recipe.

Recommended Reading

Bread Alone and **Local Breads** by Daniel Leader. From a pioneer of the artisan bread movement, lots of information and recipes for traditional European breads, along with stories of the author's travels and learning experiences in the baking world. Watch out for mathematical errors in some of the recipes.

Bread Making: A Home Course by Lauren Chattman. An excellent introduction to bread making for beginners. It covers many different types of bread, including sourdough, but is relatively short and concise. Has useful tips and information gathered from many different sources. The Q&A sections alone are worth the purchase price.

The Laurel's Kitchen Bread Book. This is a wonderful resource for whole-grain baking in general, but oddly for a whole-foods bible it does not have much information about breads raised with sourdough (its sourdough recipes usually rely on yeast to raise the bread).

King Arthur Flour Whole Grain Baking. This book has a good section on sourdough, along with many other recipes for whole grain baking (not just breads). Clear, reliable information and recipes.

Wild Sourdough by Yoke Mardewi. A vast array of exclusively sourdough bread recipes, with unusual variants including sweet as well as savory tastes, with beautiful color photographs of many of the breads. The instructions for making a starter are vague, and there are some oddities to watch out for such as strange oven temperature requirements.

The Bread Baker's Apprentice and **Peter Reinhart's Whole Grain Breads** by Peter Reinhart. Tons of information on the science and chemistry of bread, perhaps more than you want or need to know. Reinhart's recipes are interesting but very complicated. Again, he likes to use sourdough for its flavor and conditioning qualities but commercial yeast to raise his breads. He introduced me to the "soaker" concept, though, which is a brilliant way to improve whole grain breads.

Nourishing Traditions by Sally Fallon. This tome is full of information about the benefits of soaking and sprouting whole grains, a traditional practice that has become lost in our age of "convenience" foods. However, be aware that the sourdough bread recipes in this book yield a very dense, heavy bread and seem to take pride in it.

Wild Fermentation and **The Art of Fermentation** by Sandor Katz. Although these books have relatively little information about bread per se, with a broader focus on fermented foods in general, they will introduce you to the fascinating process of how those tiny organisms make so many of our most delicious, cherished and healthful foods possible. It's an age-old story that needs to become part of our consciousness again.

Sources of Supplies and Information

The Baker's Catalog

This catalog from King Arthur Flour is a great source for baking ingredients, including excellent flours, and equipment.

www.kingarthurflour.com

Bob's Red Mill

Offers a good variety of quality flours and whole grains, readily available in retail stores nationwide, or by mail order.

www.bobsredmill.com

Cultures for Health

As well as selling several types of sourdough starter (along with cultures for yogurt, kombucha, kefir and more), this site has many links, recipes and articles.

www.culturesforhealth.com

Lehman's

Based in Ohio's Amish country, Lehman's is the place for grain mills (both hand-driven and electric) and other useful and hard-to-find tools.

www.lehmans.com

National Cooperative Grocers Association

Find a cooperatively run food store near you, and learn about the social and economic benefits of the co-op model.

www.ncga.coop

Appendix:
Baking Day

This essay originally appeared in LILIPOH, Fall 2013

For a long time, bread scared me. Not the plastic-wrapped loaves I found on the grocery store shelves, but the idea of making this most elemental food myself, in my own kitchen. I was a late learner when it came to cooking, spending years heating up jarred spaghetti sauce or chicken noodle soup and calling it dinner. Even after I had mastered marinara and made my own stock from scratch, though, I still couldn't imagine baking a loaf of bread. Wasn't yeast terribly temperamental? What if I made it too warm or too cold? How would I know how long to knead the dough? What if I spent all that time and energy and ended up with a brick, or a pancake?

When I finally got my hands into a lump of dough, I had my first inkling that this bread business might not be so terrifying after all. As I took a turn at kneading a loaf made by a friend, I remember thinking "So this is what it feels like." Just a few minutes of experience wiped out years of what-ifs. Finally I was ready to try, my fears conquered by the fascination of a substance so mysteriously capable of transforming itself.

I didn't realize it at the time, but it was a good thing I was getting some practice at transformation. I was pregnant with my first child, and about to enter into a whole new realm of experience that held no room for "what-ifs."

A bowl on the counter holds a strange, spongy substance. From small amounts of flour, water, and yeast, combined and left to rest, this bubbly goo has arisen overnight. I add more water, yeast, and flour, and turn the contents of the bowl out onto the counter. I plunge my hands into the sticky mess.

The first weeks and months after the birth of my son were not easy. I was not ready for the terrifying responsbility of an infant, a helpless, voiceless creature who depended on me for his every need. My safe, predictable life was shattered, dissolved into a mess made up of my own feelings of inadequacy. Not yet knowing how to read my son's signals, suddenly bereft of the security of words, I was frequently to be found sobbing, "I don't know what to do!"

Slowly, I learned that it didn't matter that I didn't know what to do. I had to do something, and pay attention, and try again. My baby continued to survive my incompetence, and something wonderful even began to happen. A person was being born.

Pressing, turning, and folding, gradually adding more flour, I work through every bit of the damp, slimy mass. For a long time it doesn't change much. Only once my hands are getting tired does a subtle difference begin to be felt. Pressing on, I feel the dough coming together, becoming a unity. Where it had yielded helplessly to my fingers, now it begins to press back.

With all our focus on the dramatic, miraculous moment of physical birth, we forget that birth doesn't happen at one point in time. It unfolds through many stages as the individual who wishes to inhabit a tiny newborn body takes hold of it more and more, learning to stand, to speak, to say "I am here." There are countless births as a child begins to become himself or herself, pressing back against the world.

At first my son did not press back very hard. According to charts and diagrams, he was late in holding up his head, rolling over, crawling. In doctor's offices and therapy sessions I was introduced to dismaying terms like "extreme head lag" and "low tone." I saw my child being made into a statistic — specialists debated, as if it really mattered, whether his delay was twenty-five or thirty percent. They pushed and pulled at his tiny body, poking and prodding, without visible results.

I heard voices that wanted to make me anxious and unsure, and that once I would have been all too willing to listen to. But something told me that there was nothing to be gained by anxiety, nothing to do but wait. I waited.

I form the dough, now smooth and elastic, into a ball and place it in a large bowl. Covering it with a damp cloth, I set it aside in a quiet, warm place. A couple of hours later, I uncover the bowl and find the dough has grown and changed. It no longer presses back against my finger, but is receptive and relaxed, ready to take on a new shape.

At around seven months old, Brendan's first tooth appeared. Shortly thereafter, he rolled over for the first time. From then on, his progress was steady: pulling up, sitting, crawling. He spent a long time trolling the edges of the room, holding on to the furniture. But having seen what had already happened, I knew this was no cause for concern. He was taking his time, and whatever time it took was right.

I shape the dough into a firm ball and again set it aside to grow and change. When it once more accepts the imprint of a finger, it is ready to go into the oven for a final, dramatic metamorphosis.

When Brendan took his first steps, he fell down — but he was laughing in delight. It wasn't long before he was walking, not to mention running, galloping and climbing. The wisdom within him had brought about this miracle, without any instruction. And as I witnessed this, something in me had also changed. I had found that for all my preoccupation with my own accomplishments, there is something else that needs to come not from me but through me, that asks not only for hard work but also for holding back.

The baker does not create a loaf of bread. She brings together substances, supplies the strength of her hands, creates a warm and stable environment, and watches for the right moment to introduce something new. But without the invisible activity within the dough, all that work would be in vain. To be truly aware of this cannot help but call forth our awe and gratitude.

The bread is done, the loaf golden and fragrant. We break it with thanks, and all the work, time, and energy it has consumed becomes part of us again, part of the cycle of life. The will to create gives rise to the capacity to create, endlessly.

I learned something from baking bread about how to be a mother, but the process went the other way too. Before I had Brendan, I tended to bake infrequently and hesitantly, fearing mistakes, needing recipes. Since having him, I have baked more and more often — about once a week now. It hasn't always turned out as I would wish. There have been shapeless loaves and tasteless loaves, batches of dough that wouldn't rise and batches that overflowed the pan.

But if falling down can be the funniest joke in the world, then I can take my own mistakes more lightly. I've learned to feel into the dough, its varying temperament and needs, with more confidence in my own judgment and less dependence on others' opinions. I've learned to let go of words, when they get in the way of seeing what is before my eyes.

And so I have come to understand how some of the most mundane things in life can become touchstones for the sacred. Patience and presence, rhythm and rest — these are the gifts of baking day, and every day.